I0534833

BATHTUB POEMS

drum beats on a typewriter

Jerome Berglund

Setu Publications, USA

Bathtub Poems

By
Jerome Berglund

Setu Publications

* Pittsburgh, PA (USA) *

© 2023 by Jerome Berglund

ISBN-13 (paperback): 978-1-947403-24-6

Distributed to the book trade worldwide by Setu Publications, Pittsburgh (USA)

All rights reserved. No part of this work may be reproduced, translated, recorded, stored, transmitted, or displayed in any form, or by any means electronic, mechanical, or otherwise without the prior written permission of the author, the copyright owner except for brief quotations in book reviews, and as otherwise permitted by applicable law. Any such quotations must acknowledge the source.

We would be pleased to receive email correspondence regarding this publication or related topics at setuedit@gmail.com.

Although every precaution has been taken in the preparation of this work, neither the author nor the publisher shall have any liability to any person or entity with respect to any loss or damage caused or alleged to be caused directly or indirectly by the information contained in this work.

Cover Art: The Customs Post by Henri Rousseau, c1890, oil on canvas

Material previously published in:

Asahi Shimbun, Bear Creek Haiku, Better Than Starbucks, Bubble, Danse Macabre, Equinox, Erato, Fresh Out Magazine, Haiku Dialogue, Hooghly Review, Hive Avenue, Ink Pantry, Lothlorien Poetry Journal, miniMAG, North Dakota Quarterly Otoliths, Poetry As Promised, Roadside Raven Review, Stanza Cannon, Synchronized Chaos, Winnetka-Northfield Library Short Poetry Contest, Zen Space

BATHTUB POEMS

drum beats on a typewriter

Jerome Berglund

to Jack Ashford, Dave Hamilton, James
Gittens, and Jack Brokensha

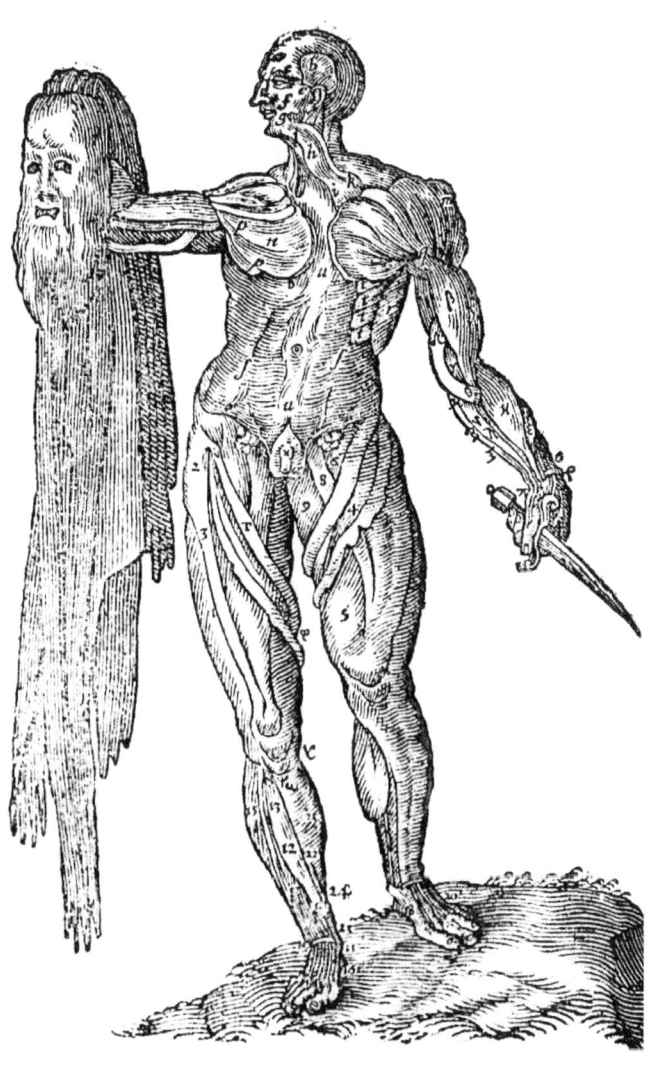

contents

Après moi, le déluge

0

clear sky —
inside a pin cushion
looking out

0

solid waste
scrawled on grubby mattress
strewn across dirt-clod laden sidewalk

0

fugitive year drags on
spring becomes winter's apex
still hear hounds baying

0

at the Princess Depot

light-rail crossing sounds noisily
beyond the concrete divider garlanded,
wreathed with verdigris, vines of ivy
spectral figures in garters, coats and tails
or high-collared, bustle
and flitter about on parade,
make their way to picnics
to see an alligator, a mountain lion,
primates in the menagerie
parasols protecting their anemic
pale complexions
from the late September sun's onslaught
red battered bricks read Flint Co.
a ladybug floats
drifts
putters past

0

tall hills of glossy powder
call to mind Hopewell burial mounds,
    earthworks

0

unpaid meter
sitting in someone else's car –
    stare around nervously

0

surround ourselves
with beautiful things, soaps unopened
    instruments we can't play

0

more comfortable
in company of shades these days
than the living breathing

0

washing crockery
is hard in the dark, go by feel
rely on texture

0

faded trains, rusty tags
repose on withdrawn tracks
just off 44th

0

sucker

when she couldn't recognize
a single one of us any longer
or get out of that wheelchair
bathe on her own
draped in adult undergarments
my grandmother made these
framed coloring book squares
sloppily filled in with bright neon colors
occasionally spilling over the lines
of the words:
'TODAY IS GOING TO BE AWESOME'
gave one to each person in our family
now they are positioned strategically
about all of their homes
and whenever I glimpse one unprepared
it slaps me like an open palm
hard across the face
and I cannot help but remember
how near the end she was always
compulsively singing that song,
among the only things she any longer
could rightly remember
solemnly but perhaps
somewhere deep below
where her prodigious cognizance lay buried
with scathing, bitter irony too
like a lamentation or accusation
a plea for rescue, deliverance:
'*Jesus loves me*', that lullaby
'*This I know, for the Bible tells me so*'
and that's what I think about optimism

0

it gets quite foggy here
when the ice melts up
a painterly haze

0

compulsions of cleanliness
and the Hegel
swivels away from

0

hear borealis
was hiding behind the clouds again
this gray night

0

wetted leaves long since vanished
leave pronounced imprint
as benefaction

0

lone seat
casts a long shadow
o'er snow in the lamplight

0

drooping nepeta
prostrated as though mourning
before a grave site

0

trampled spot center of pot
where calico reclined
since departed

0

sunny sill
carrot tops submerged in jigger glasses
New World war trophies

0

cat meowing
through neighboring door, I'd feed you
if I were able to

0

oxidation
bubbles around wheel wells
like venereal disease

0

guided meditation

always feels like I'm being violated
in a ritualized, carefully plotted manner
maybe it's tone of the voice
soothing, authoritative making demands
I'm uncomfortable with
but cannot comfortably extricate
myself from the authority
control, clutches of
must grit my teeth
steel spirit and bear it
hold breath, wait out
'let the day's clenched fist
release as you allow yourself
to breathe in relaxation
those areas of tension subside'
assailant whispers
like gaucho breaking a bronco
with placations, calming consoling
telling me to touch myself
feel loosening my jaw area and tongue
business I want no part of

0

     as though God is ashing
his great cigar upon me
     flicks spackle my coat

0   *Otoliths, March 2022*

     there's something coercive
in forced rhyming, one presses
     adhere to a scheme

0

     at night
the decayed floorboards
     creak much more prominently

Ice Floe, July 2022

0

when audiences catch
errors in playing, imagine
how many they miss

0   *Roadside Raven, July 2022*

shoveling technique
degenerates after a few weeks
without an avalanche

0

exposure
to elements, the rusting's
fractious catalyst

0

time ravages
a frying pan never touched water
dirt keeps the funk

0

consent to keep edge honed
but can't make me care much
about the handle

0

may minimize
noise or splashing, but not both
at the same time

0

there is something onerous and intimidating

about chapters advancing unnumbered
seemingly without marker or guidepost
like a pristine workhouse wall
without benefit of notchings implemented
to track our passage through the temporal
devoid landmarks and turning points
milestone or lodestar

0

snowfall
is hardest to contend with
when it comes upon one slowly

0

as each day dims
am flickering lit, skin alternates
between green and blue

0

finicky
about trimming wicks, waste no energy
luminance regulated

0

window by commode
must secure your blinds,
hide this pissing about

0

    panoply of lines intersecting
carve through glop
    jerkwater islands

0

    the days snow doesn't stick
isn't visible, but chill remains
    feel colder

0

the midday sun setting

bathes chamber in macchiato
I butterfly stroke through flood's torrents
this current immersion
towards exit for a gulp
of less fusty, tainted air
like freshwater fish
stumbled into the salty ocean

0

when more blizzards
are projected, makes sense waiting
to clear for the time being

0

smoker in flurry
a derelict bust
begging for feather dusting

0

leaning against
this poorly seated, wobbly post
it's real hard to write straight

0

months of puffing
on a leaf pile without incident;
horripilation

0

violet trim
on windows of white house
certainly makes a statement

0

flopped upside down
the battered amazon box
now displays a long frown

0

running in the background,
too many applications
draining battery

0

gooseflesh in lukewarm tub
ice-water from spigot
heater depleted

0

why does advent calendar
feel like time-bomb counting down,
fuse hiss to dynamite

0

can avoid Trouble
for a time, but it's a patient one
is bound to catch up

"The suit on the chimp."

- Valerie Solanas

Vulcanalia

0

    dreamt I lost a moon in time
which I learned
    had been rather eventful

0

    through the trees
it looks like our city
    is on fire this strange Sunday

North Dakota Quarterly, February 2023

0

I hope you never find yourself

in the parlor scene
when Jimmy Stewart gets revealed
to be the disturbed, conniving
murderous criminal mastermind
behind it all – the discord, infamy –
and become tasked with
trying to make sense of things
stooping down low
to scoop up and collect
the snow globe's many
iridescent shattered pieces

0

when you pull e-brake
can't grouse about
        consequences of misadventure

0

steep, disagreeable
entry fee it takes…
        get certain select places

0

retire shaver's blade
only once begins to rake flesh
        draws first blood

0

look down and see face
branded waffle iron, flood lamp
switches off abruptly

0

the good boss uses
a pneumatic pistol
to deliver sack
no warning instantaneous
scuffed floors, red-letter days

0

crack of dawn
after full night without sun
makes for coldest time of day

0

fuzzy lops might yearn for release from captivity

escape to the great outdoors
but watching a bony hare shivering
beneath tree in the pounding sleet
know they're better off
despite drawbacks
flies in the ointment

0

icicle sticks out of the ground –
a bolt of Jove's
just landed

0

gnat pressed between palms
breaks down into multitude
of subsections

0

in emergency room
every day is *de los muertes*
and all saints

0

stage your breakdown
existential crises
somewhere picturesque
that photographs well
if you want any to invest in it

Fresh Out Magazine, May 2022

0

Tennessee recognizes
only productive way
to spend a sabbatical

0

removed comforter
too early, still drying out
so now I quiver

0

an engine revving impatiently

other vehicles with lights dimmed
swiftly pulling out,
speeding away in all directions
figures darting through
harsh shadows of lanterns
some inscrutable criminality afoot
which nonplusses me
when I've no part in it

0

yard is asbestos
popcorn ceiling inverted
foam party doomsday

0

prepare to enter
chainsaw pattern, sin wave
of volatility

0

powder everywhere
from all this fervid baking
best not to wear black

0

remove a motor's limiter
at own hazard, leaves nothing
to check it

0

tabula rasa:
blank sky through grimy window;
anhedonia

0

the bait says,
*'here's why you don't stand in the road
after an accident'*

0

ripper weather

out there in the alleyway
beneath the street lamps
a dangerous time
to be a stray pet
about this foggy city
at night

0

limp, dangling
basketball net
   crudely strung up

0

   types out in these conditions
prefer not to be...
   little choice in the matter

0

insular Tudor
your story has been written
on sodden parchment

0

it feels later
when gets dark so much earlier
the days are shorter

0

squirrel scrabbling
across power line, I hope that you
know what you're doing

0

well-shaken Jumex
on gelid day
approximates banana split

0

a hangman in pink chalk

cheerfully suspended on the asphalt
near Minnehaha, a stone's throw from
short distance to Mankato
in the scheme of things
on Dakota land
country belonged to the Sioux nation

0

the concrete sidewalk
eats its way through fresh snow
while grass stays blanketed

0

predicament
to reflect on, resignation
flatly rejected

Hooghly Review, December 2022

0

cold and hot
fluid coalesce, equal hair-raising
in their ways

0

selvportrett lancing boils
pockmarked topography
lunar rove maria

Hive Avenue, May 2022

0

slices of rippling orange fizzles
framed in tan wood
distressed, cottagecore

0

sunset paints trees
ghastly bucketful
red latex tincture

0

furball died last month

but I swear tonight
I heard its ghost mewling
through quiescence
couldn't have been
the puss had lived below
never got a chance to meet
its having also quit
with the previous lodgers
weeks ago, and all the furniture since
steam-cleaned at great expense
so not a trace of clumped hair
any longer remains

0

when feline has croaked
small consolation
    it was not on your watch

0

more dwindled
circle of acquaintance gets
    the less holiday shopping

Danse Macabre, May 2022

0

a desiccated
mummy's character, has the birch
and its dressings

0

parishioner slides
in kirk parking lot… but does not go down
rights self

0

jade, ochre, carmine
a triumvirate incarnate
of arboretum

0

December rain stings
but know with few degrees shaved
it could be so much worse

0

returning to the municipal garden

I find the flowers have all
made themselves scarce,
clean dirt remains
giving no indication
they had ever passed through
and we are left wondering
where they have gone
whether were disposed of
or huddle beside
a warm space heater
through the chill
winter months,
if they'll e'er be
replanted again

0

Protégé resembles
a powdered donut, guess this
is happening again

0

the year is scented
with overpowering carnations
a smell hard to get out

Synchronized Chaos, *April 2022*

0

when corrosive chemicals
long flowed through, being in rough shape
is understandable

0

summer shower
washes caked grime off of finish
shrovetide, paisen monday

0

she broke the string

pendent pull-chain off and
unsure how to proceed
just left the bare naked bulb
burning day and night
having no other recourse
immediately on hand
in her wheelhouse
and that pantry stayed bright
for weeks on end
to collective astonishment
indeed has not burnt out yet

0

indomitable
dry ice block keeps on steaming
even in worst heat

0

spontaneous interpretive dancer
really adds
to composition

0

cracked screen gives character
tell myself, trademarks
all my equipage collect

Lothlorien, April 2022

Hive Avenue, May 2022

0

retches activated charcoal
the picture
of a sorry soul possessed

0   *Hive Avenue, May 2022*

must become parched
for water to taste good, famished
savor day-old crust

0

can tumbler stick the landing
close strong with flying colors...
tune in to find out

Hive Avenue, May 2022

"I never thought of profit, rather of loss."

- Charles Armitage Brown

Ecclesia poenitens

0

life's latter portion
invariably becomes
a salvage operation

0

entryway bookends
reap-time cubed shrubbery
suggest the red sea

0

I walk out and greet a world

that seems inanimate
like have missed the rapture
and all remaining is still
as an array of façades on a film set
but for the relaxed scuttling
of a few scattered, crunchy leaves
the hardwood trees nod along
to a refrain I cannot hear

0

first cigarette of the day
in November, quake like alley-cat
frosted windshield

0

with gorilla glue
attempt to bond cuff-link
of Thaddeus together

0

kind of chapped feet
could be washed pornographically
in a photo-op

0

brisk is perfectly
alright, can bear so long as
there remains sunshine

0

in keening imbecile
across aisle
see myself through others' eyes

0

tombstones in the snow
emerge like porpoises
surfacing from endless

Erato, August 2022

0

patterned curtains
are transparent in the moonbeam...
newborn with a caul

0

scrape tennis on edge of steps
but still leave fine white trail
across runner

0

sense of daring
in traversing defunct railways
despite loneliness

0

sister pink presides
over Pentecost with patience;
first snow

0

watch blue jeopardy squares
cascade across street –
which of us more piteous

0

cramming stacks of bootlegged cassette tapes

from the old video store days
and my stint at Blockbuster
into the bin, jamming them under
yellowed magazines with
a gap-toothed ginger scamp
fooling across their covers
wrongdoings of a bygone era
wonder if they're even worth covering up
but I still go through the motions
out of habit

0

installing ink cartridge
smeared thumb shakes me,
to shamed remembrances

0

security feature
prevents locking while warms up
vulnerability

Erato, August 2022

0

untroubled by wax
focus on cultivating those raw combs;
muqarnas

0

the comfort
of a downcycle, no investments
need worry about cashing

0

dark and deep waters
below surface... whose bottom
would not care to sound

0

solar lamps
which have stored energy, can light path
if placed cleverly

0

Gulliver's god
has returned to its temple again
issues jubilant ticks

0

how much
are the roots absorbing
what is being evaporated

0

a white cockatiel

shyly said hello,
then volunteered softly
that she loved me;
but alas I would not be the one
to get her out of that cage,
why I generally avoid
such dismal places
charming though their captive
specimens may prove

0

    poinsettia's petal
is impeccably perky
      so place it back beside pistil

0

    go ahead and steal my ride…
you can be the one
      broke down by side of road

0

don't have any good luck charms
now that I think of it;
plant heather early

0

Henry David
at rainbow's terminus
filling pockets with pyrite

Zen Space, August 2022

0

these icicles
on my wagon worry…
but who travels in winter

0

yellow tree:
steady drip-dropping water torture
keep coming back, rake

Asahi Shimbun, November 2022

0

S 42nd Avenue

an orgy of efflorescence in every distinction,
teaming riotously, draped in gowns
of all the silken colors on the spectrum
merrily careening, cavorting, pirouetting
drunkenly to a waltz, a polka
a chanson by Béranger
in 6/8 time

Danse Macabre, May 2022

0

what's those birds chirping,
she asks on other end of the line
midwinter

0

ma ties
an old lady's shoelace
and off she waddles confidently

Bear Creek Haiku, April 2022

Asahi Shimbun, June 2022

0

sundays no one's
on the road, never difficult
getting in to church

0

when toddling and disabled
are permitted
things get wonderfully noisy

0

gospel songs emerge sleepily
out of muscle memory
yawning

0

coupé never moves now
serves merely as something
to rest on, escritoire

0

searching for Rat Park
been trying to find way there
since cannot remember

0

I like it when the old-timers
put their hands up
in the air

Asahi Shimbun, June 2022

acknowledgements

I am grateful to the editors of the following magazines and anthologies in which some of these poems or earlier versions of them first appeared:

Asahi Shimbun: "cat meowing", "yellow tree", "sundays", "old-timers";
Bear Creek Haiku: "shoelace";
Better Than Starbucks: "slowly";
Bubble: "branded";
Danse Macabre "birds chirping", "holiday shopping";
Equinox: "midday sun";
Erato: "endless", "muqarnas", "vulnerability";
Fresh Out Magazine: "existential";
Haiku Dialogue: "pin cushion";
Hive Avenue: "lancing", "activated charcoal", "become parched", "tune in";
The Hooghly Review: "resignation";
Ice Floe Press: "floorboards"'
Ink Pantry "rough shape";
Lothlorien Poetry Journal: "cracked screen";
miniMAG: "S 42ⁿᵈ Ave"'
North Dakota Quarterly: "strange Sunday";
Otoliths: "forced rhyming";
Poetry As Promised: "municipal garden", "find yourself", "fuzzy lops";
Roadside Raven Review: "shoveling technique";
Stanza Cannon: "princess depot", "onerous";
Synchronized Chaos: "carnations";
Winnetka-Northfield Library Poetry Contest: "white cockatiel";
Zen Space: "Henry David".

A graduate of the
University of Southern California's
Cinema-Television Production program,
Jerome Berglund spent a picaresque
decade in the entertainment industry
before returning to the Midwest
where he was born and raised.
They nabbed him at Occupy Los Angeles;
he eluded capture at Standing Rock.
His recent and forthcoming writing
publications include short stories
in *Grim & Gilded*, *Stardust*,
and the *Watershed Review*,
a play in *Iris Literary Journal*,
and poetry in *Asahi Shimbun*,
Failed Haiku, and *Scarlet Dragonfly*.
He is also an established,
award-winning fine art photographer,
whose black and white
pictures have been exhibited
in New York, Minneapolis,
and Santa Monica galleries.

www.ingramcontent.com/pod-product-compliance
Lightning Source LLC
Chambersburg PA
CBHW061258170626
46811CB00015BA/3103